BIBLE
101

SIX SESSIONS FOR SMA[...]

PERSONAL DEVOTION

Taking God's
Word to heart

WILLOW CREEK RESOURCES

kathy dice
BILL DONAHUE, SERIES EDITOR

ivp

InterVarsity Press
Downers Grove, Illinois
Leicester, England

InterVarsity Press
P.O. Box 1400, Downers Grove, IL 60515
World Wide Web: www.ivpress.com
E-mail: mail@ivpress.com

Inter-Varsity Press, England
38 De Montfort Street, Leicester LE1 7GP, England

InterVarsity Press® is the book-publishing division of InterVarsity Christian Fellowship/USA®, a student movement active on campus at hundreds of universities, colleges and schools of nursing in the United States of America, and a member movement of the International Fellowship of Evangelical Students. For information about local and regional activities, write Public Relations Dept., InterVarsity Christian Fellowship/USA, 6400 Schroeder Rd., P.O. Box 7895, Madison, WI 53707-7895.

Inter-Varsity Press, England, is the book-publishing division of the Universities and Colleges Christian Fellowship (formerly the Inter-Varsity Fellowship), a student movement linking Christian Unions in universities and colleges throughout the United Kingdom and the Republic of Ireland, and a member movement of the International Fellowship of Evangelical Students. For information about local and national activities write to UCCF, 38 De Montfort Street, Leicester LE1 7GP.

Cover design: Grey Matter Group

Photo image: Paul Eekhoff/Masterfile

Chapter icons: Roberta Polfus

USA ISBN 0-8308-2068-X

UK ISBN 0-85111-531-4

Printed in the United States of America ∞

15	14	13	12	11	10	9	8	7	6	5	4	3	2	1
11	10	09	08	07	06	05	04	03	02	01	00			

Contents

Introduction

Some time ago, Russ Robinson (director of small group ministries at Willow Creek Community Church and concept editor on these guides) and I were talking about how to help groups get a firm grip on the Word of God. Both of us had studied and taught courses on the Bible, but what about small groups? What if we could put something together that could be studied as a group and yet have much of the information people would normally find in a class or course? Well, hats off to Russ, who came up with the idea for Bible 101 and cast the vision for what it could look like. Soon we were outlining the books, and the result is what you have before you. So welcome to the Bible 101 adventure, a place where truth meets life!

Traditionally the subject matter in this series has been reserved for classroom teaching or personal study. Both are places where this curriculum could be used. But this work is primarily targeted at small groups, places where men and women, old and young, rich and poor gather together in community to engage fully with the truth of God's Word. These little communities can be transforming in ways that classrooms and personal study cannot.

Few things in life are more fulfilling than drawing out the deep truths of Scripture and then seeing them at work to change a life into the image of Christ. Getting a firm grip on the Bible and its teachings is paramount to a mature and intelligent walk with God. We are to worship him with all our heart, soul, mind and strength. And the Word of God is central to accomplishing God's desire that we be fully devoted to him.

The team from Willow Creek—staff and volunteers alike—has labored diligently to provide you with a group-friendly process for understanding the Bible. Kathy Dice, Gerry Mathisen, Judson Poling, Michael Redding and I have worked to provide something that merges content and process, learning and application. Now it is up to you to work together to discover the riches that lie ahead for those willing to do some work and take a few risks. But we know you are more than ready for that challenge!

To make these studies more productive, here are a few suggestions and guidelines to help you along the way. Read carefully so that you get the most out of this series.

Purpose
This series is designed to ground a Christ-follower in the study and understanding of Scripture. It is not designed for someone who became a Christian last week, though sections of it would certainly be good. And it is not as rigorous as a Bible college class or seminary course might be. Bible 101 means *foundational,* but not easy or light. So be prepared for some challenge and some stretching. This may be the first time you are exposed to certain theological concepts or terms, or to some more in-depth methods of Bible study. Celebrate the challenge and strive to do your best. Peter tells us to "make every effort" to add knowledge to our faith. It will take some effort, but I can guarantee it will be well worth it!

Prayer
When approaching the Word of God you will need to keep a submissive and teachable attitude. The Holy Spirit is eager to teach you, but you must be willing to receive knowledge, encouragement, correction and challenge. One educator has taught that all learning is the result of failed expectations. We hope that in some ways you are ambushed by the truth and stumble upon new and unfamiliar territory that startles you into new ways of thinking about God and relating to him through Christ.

Practice
Each session has the same format, except (in some cases) the last session. For five meetings you will learn skills, discuss material and readings, work together as a team, and discover God's truths in fresh and meaningful ways. The sixth session will be an opportunity to put all you have learned into practice. Studies are designed as follows.

Establishing Base Camp (5-10 minutes). A question or icebreaker to focus the meeting.

 Mapping the Trail (5-10 minutes). An overview of where we are headed.

 Beginning the Ascent (30 minutes). The main portion of the discussion time.

Gaining a Foothold (3 minutes). Information to read that identifies core issues and ideas to keep you on track with the journey.

 Trailmarkers (10 minutes). Important Scriptures for memorization or reflection.

 Teamwork (15 minutes). A group activity (sometimes done in subgroups) to build community and share understanding of what was learned.

 Reaching the Summit (5 minutes). A chance to summarize and look back at what has been learned or accomplished.

Close in Prayer (as long as you want!). An opportunity to pray for one another and ask God to deepen the truths of Scripture in you.

You can take some shortcuts or take longer as the group decides, but strive to stay on schedule for a 75- to 90-minute meeting, including prayer time. You will also want to save time to attend to personal needs. This will vary by group and can also be accomplished in personal relationships you develop between meetings.

Preparation

Preparation? There is none! Well, almost none. For some sessions reading ahead will be suggested to provide an overview. But the sessions are designed to be worked through together. We find this builds a sense of team and community, and is also more fun! And there is something about "discovery in the moment" rather than merely discussing what everyone has already discovered outside the meeting that provides a sense of adventure.

We wish you the best as you draw truth from the Word of God for personal transformation, group growth and kingdom impact!

Bill Donahue, Series Editor
Vice President, Small Group Ministries
Willow Creek Association

Session 1

Devotional Reading
God's Word to Me

Establishing Base Camp

Every summer as I was growing up, my family took a two-week vacation to a cottage on a lake in northern Michigan. It was great fun. Mom would splash around with us. Dad would toss us off his shoulders and teach us how to swim underwater. In the evenings he read us stories or made up some wild tale. It was the best two weeks of the year.

When I became a teenager, the highlight of the weeks shifted—my focus was on receiving letters from my boyfriend. Mostly the letters were the kind of mushy love letters only young teenagers can write. I went to my bedroom where I could be alone and read them over and over, slowly, pausing now and then to decipher his handwriting and to contemplate his words. My young heart would do flip-flops as I thought about the day I'd get back home and we could talk again. Although we didn't say all those mushy words in person, when we were separated it was nice to know he missed me. Those letters were our connection, our means of communication, our relational link.

✓ Think of a time you received a letter from someone important in your life, maybe a love letter or a letter asking for your forgiveness or offering you forgiveness. Maybe a letter with good news or perhaps a letter with sad news. What were your thoughts and feelings? Describe your experience.

Mapping the Trail

The Bible is a letter to us from God. Sometimes it has good news, sometimes sad news. Sometimes it is matter-of-fact. Sometimes it is instructional. It is a love letter revealing his heart. There are stories and poetry, history lessons and parables. We can read it quickly on the run, or we can choose to read it slowly, trying to understand what God is saying specifically to us.

✓ How often do you read the Bible? Why do you read it, or why don't you read it?

✓ What parts of the Bible do you enjoy reading? What parts do you stay away from reading? Why?

✓ What is your style of reading the Bible? (For example, do you like to sit and ponder what you have read, or do you read it quickly and take its thoughts with you into your day?)

Beginning the Ascent

Growing up in a pastor's home, I often heard how important it was for Christians to have "devotions," a "quiet time" for reading the Bible and praying. When I was fourteen years old, I decided to try this. I set the alarm clock for fifteen minutes before my usual time of getting up. I spent those extra fifteen minutes reading a chapter in the Bible and praying. I must confess that not very often did I get a special message from God, but I was proud of myself for having devotions. Perhaps the most important lesson I learned at that early age was how much God wanted to meet with me.

My house was on the way to school for some of my friends. They came to my house, and we walked the rest of the way together. I was habitually late. When I started meeting with God, I remember saying, "Lord, if I do this for you would you help me be ready for school on time?" From the morning I started meeting with God in my childlike, simple way, I was never late again. I can't explain it, but it made a deep impression on my young heart. God answered my prayer. My spending time with him in his Word was important to him.

In those days I would choose a book of the Bible, quickly read a chapter (hoping it was short) and pray for help for myself and my family. Through the years I have come to appreciate different approaches to Bible reading. Sometimes I will read only one verse and meditate on it. Other times I will read only the few verses that focus on one theme or story. Sometimes I will read a chapter and sometimes several chapters. But my favorite way to read Scripture is to read it devotionally. I read a passage, ponder its meaning for my life, read it several more times and let it soak into my soul. I think about the God who inspired the text and talk to him about it. Why did he say this? What does he want to say to me in it?

Reading the Bible devotionally means reading it as a lover reads a love letter—with the heart, with an open mind and with the attitude of a learner. It is reading the Bible slowly to hear God's special message to you. The purposes of studying the Bible are analysis and knowledge as well as application. The purpose of reading devotionally is to listen to God's heart of love for you. Life is noisy with stress and confusion. Hearing God's heart of love quiets the noise and brings peace to our innermost being.

When I began "having devotions," it was like putting in my time to read the Bible and pray. Since learning how to read the Bible devotionally, I come to the Bible with my heart, not my clock. Devotional reading reveals the heart of God. You will see God with the inner eyes of your soul. The false wisdom of this world will become clear as God's true wisdom fills your mind. You will fall in love with the Lord over and over, more and more deeply, as you pause to hear his special words to you. The message of the Bible will begin to reside in your soul.

How to Read Devotionally

Read slowly, quietly, word for word.

Read from the heart with your emotions and feelings as well as with your mind and thoughts.

Pause periodically and allow the truth of a passage to reach your soul.

Look for an insight into human life and into your life.

Prayerfully ask God for his message to you.

Keep a record of God's message and your thoughts. Be sure the message is true to God's nature, God's Word, God's will and the content of the passage. You may want to keep a spiritual journal in which you write the date of the reading, the reference and your response.

✓ As a group, read Psalm 23 devotionally, following the guidelines above and looking for personal treasures as listed below.

Treasures to Look For in Devotional Reading

1. A personal message. God knows what you are facing. Often as we read the Bible, God speaks directly to our need.

2. A promise from God. The Bible has many universal promises that apply to every believer of every generation. Watch for these promises. Be aware that not every passage has a promise, nor is every promise universal. Some promises are specific to the occasion and for people they were written to. Watch for any conditions to this promise. Ask how this promise can apply to you.

3. A command from God. All God's commands are for our good. However, remember that some of the commandments, especially in the Old Testament, were specifically for the nation of Israel. Consider whether there is a commandment for you in the passage.

> Our spiritual life is enhanced by communication with God. Reading the Bible devotionally will bring us into his majesty and his love. We will hear his message to us individually. Sometimes you may not want to follow an agenda. Just let God speak to you as he desires.

4. A timeless principle. This is a statement that fits life in any age and guides us in decision-making and character development.

5. A personal application. What difference does this passage mean for your life today and tomorrow?

Gaining a Foothold

E. Stanley Jones, a missionary to the Hindus and Muslims of India in the first half of the twentieth century, wrote, "No Christian is sound who is not scriptural" (quoted in *Devotional Classics*, edited by Richard J. Foster and James Bryan Smith). Make it a habit to read the Bible devotionally. While Bible study helps us know why a passage was written and how it applies to life today, reading the Bible devotionally brings an added dimension as God's Word enters your heart and not just your mind.

Trailmarkers

Read Psalm 19:7-11; Psalm 119:97-105; John 15:7.
Consider memorizing one of these verses.

✓ What do these passages say to you about the Scriptures?

✓ What will the Scriptures do for you?

Teamwork

Read Psalm 103. Follow the guidelines for how to read devotionally listed under "Beginning the Ascent." Ask the questions in the "Treasures to Look For" section. Begin a spiritual journal with your answers. Although reading devotionally is best done in solitude and not always with a list of questions, listening to the heart-thoughts of the others in your group will enhance your own emotions and thoughts as you begin this style of reading the Bible.

Reaching the Summit

Reading the Bible devotionally provides opportunity to devote your love, appreciation and worship to God, and to receive his love and affirmation back. Try scheduling fifteen or thirty minutes a day, a week or a month on your calendar when you can sit in a quiet place to read the Bible devotionally. Do this when your mind is fresh. Morning works for many people. But evening is fine too if that works best for you. Begin by asking God to help you free your mind from the distractions of life and to concentrate on meeting with him in his Word. Take a few minutes to think about your devotional reading pattern.

Next Session

In this session we have considered how to read the Bible devotionally in order to hear what God is saying to us. In our next session we will consider our response to him and his message.

Read as much of 1 John as possible. It is a short but profound letter. Watch for the ways we can show our love back to God.

Close in Prayer

Thank God for his love and for revealing it to you through his Word. Pray for group members to hear what God might be saying to each one individually this next week as you read 1 John.

Session 2

A Well-Ordered Heart
My Response to God

Establishing Base Camp

For centuries people have expressed love in hope that others would receive it as it was meant. However, many times the expression of love has not been received as the giver had wished. Husbands and wives, parents and children get frustrated when love is extended and there is no positive response.

Recently people have begun to ask others, "What is your love language?" so that they can show their love in meaningful ways and have it received as love. I asked my teenage niece what her love language is, and her response was, "Spend time with me and buy me things." A friend of mine asked her teenage son the same question. His answer was similar, "Buy me things." When I ask parents how they would like to be shown love from their children, their answer is quite universal: "I'd love it if my children would obey me on the first request."

This is important not only in the home but also in the workplace. How can an employer express appreciation so that it is received in a positive way? And how can an employee express gratefulness so that the boss understands? Knowing each other's love language empowers us to express and experience love as it is intended.

✓ From the list on page 15, identify your love language(s). Think of when you feel loved and appreciated. Now, how would you like your spouse, children, parents, friends, boss or employees to express love to you? How does it feel to be loved in ways meaningful to you?

Love Languages (from *The Five Love Languages* by Gary Chapman)
Giving gifts
Physical touch
Acts of service
Quality time
Words of affirmation

Mapping the Trail

As we saw in the last session, God loves us very much, so much in fact that he died to make our salvation possible. The Bible is God's message to us revealing his love. His dealings with us on a daily basis flow freely out of his extravagant love for us. We have the opportunity to express love back to God.

✓ How do you feel when God expresses love to you?

✓ How do you express your love to God?

Beginning the Ascent

The Bible is very clear regarding who God is and what our relationship with him should be like. In Matthew 6 Jesus taught his disciples to pray. They were to address God as "Our Father in heaven." John 1:12 tells us that all who trust Jesus as their personal Savior are considered children of God. Romans 8:14-17 tells us that God has adopted us into his family and we can call him "Dearest Father." In fact the Holy Spirit continually reminds us that we are children of God. Along with being adopted as children into God's family, we will receive his inheritance for all eternity upon our entrance into his home in heaven.

According to Colossians 2:9, all the fullness of God lives in Jesus in bodily form. In other words, Jesus is God in the flesh. By looking at the life of Jesus we understand God and how he values us. First, we notice that Jesus often left the crowds and went alone to pray, to talk with his Father in heaven (Luke 6:12; Matthew 14:23). Before coming to earth in bodily form, Jesus had experienced perfect community with God the Father in heaven. While he was physically separated from God, Jesus talked with his Father often. At the end of his life, he prayed a final prayer for his followers (John 17). In this prayer we see a second way that Jesus set an example for us—while on earth Jesus had done what the Father asked him to do. Also, in John 15:10 Jesus tells us that he abided in the Father's love by obeying the Father's commandments.

Depending on our experience as children growing up in our individual families, or as parents of our own children, our view of the benefits of spending time with and obeying a parent may differ. Some years ago I was asked to consider interviewing for an influential volunteer leadership position in my church. At the time, my aging father lived with me and he felt I shouldn't seek this position. Because of his health and the stress my accepting this position would cause, I declined the honor being offered to me. This was one of the hardest decisions I had ever made. It didn't seem right or fair that I, an adult, should give up such a special opportunity just because my father requested that I not do it.

A few days after I declined, God helped me realize that Christ gave up the glories of heaven and suffered the wounds of the cross at his Father's request. Wow! I had been given an experience much like Jesus had, to obey his father or to follow his own desires. The benefit came some months later when I was asked to join the paid staff of my church, a position much more suited to who I am and my passions for ministry. I found out later that the way I honored my father was a major factor when leaders of the church considered me for the staff position. An additional benefit was in my relationship with my father for his remaining years. As I followed in his footsteps of church ministry, he conferred on me his mantle of blessing.

God is our ideal Father. What he asks of us is for our good. When we obey him, we are blessed. The blessing may be different from what we imagine, but it will be there. We will know the blessing of a well-ordered heart, a heart that follows after God and is at peace with him. One blessing of a well-ordered heart is feeling confident to come into his presence in prayer. Other blessings come when we read his Word, the blessings of comfort and joy in being in his family, of our sins being forgiven, of knowing his greatness that is bigger than our life, of experiencing his wisdom in decisions.

Gaining a Foothold

In 1 Samuel 8 we read that the people of God no longer wanted God to rule and guide them because he was invisible and distant. They wanted a human king who would ride before them in battle. God was sad about this because he knew a human king would be fallible and often self-centered, not leading for the benefit of the people as God had done.

Unfortunately, in our society we have given rulership of our lives to human kings, spouses, employers, parents, children, friends and coworkers. They ask us to obey them for their good, not necessarily for our good. Consequently, we have been wounded in our obedience. Obedience is seen as weak. God longs to be the king of our lives. His reign will always be for our good, according to his will. However, obedience to God is difficult because of our human perspective on obedience. Reading the transforming Word of God with an open heart and mind will allow us to see God's love in the obedience he requires of us.

Trailmarkers

Read Psalm 32:8-11 and Proverbs 3:5-8.

✓ What do these verses say to you about God's love language to us?

✓ Where do we find his guidance and wisdom? Discuss your individual thoughts regarding the meaning of these verses and their application to your personal life.

Teamwork

In pairs read 1 John 2—5. Each pair should take a different chapter. Listen for the verses that indicate God's language for receiving love from us. Make a list of the ways God knows we love him. After about ten minutes come together and briefly share with others your thoughts about each of the items on the list. You may want to also include how you are personally doing in each of these areas and in what areas you want to grow.

A well-ordered heart is a heart at peace with God and self. The way to experience this peace is to respond to God with his love language of obedience and community with him. When we are at peace with God, we will be at peace with ourselves because we will know how much God loves us and values each of us as individual children in his family.

Reaching the Summit

Briefly discuss your thoughts about the two ways Jesus showed his love to the Father and how these two demonstrations of love are also evident in your life. Then discuss who has rule over your life. How does this affect your perspective on obedience to God?

✓ How did Jesus communicate with God?

✓ How did he obey the Father's commands?

✓ How do you speak with God and obey his commands?

✓ Who is in charge of your life?

✓ How does this affect your view of obedience to God?

Next Session

In this session we have considered how to respond to God in his love language—obedience and communication. In our next session we will consider ways to treasure God's Word through Scripture memory.

Choose a verse or a few verses from 1 John that impacted you at the heart level. Use these verses for your work in the next session on memorization.

Close in Prayer

Thank God for revealing his love language to us so we don't have to guess how to please him or how to show him our love.

Pray for each person in the group by name. Focus on issues that have come up regarding each person's perspective on obedience to God's commandments, especially as stated in 1 John.

Session 3

Scripture Memory
Treasuring God's Word

 Establishing Base Camp

Recently, as some friends of mine were coming home from church, a police car and fire engine roared passed them with sirens blowing and lights flashing. My friends pulled to the side of the road to let the emergency vehicles pass, and they wondered where the fire was. Unfortunately, as they turned the corner on their street, they saw the fire and smoke billowing out of their own home. Their house, including virtually all their possessions, was lost in the fire, which had been burning for an hour before anyone noticed or called for help. The next day as they sifted through the ashes, they came across some photo albums that somehow had survived the inferno. The reminders of good times and family memories were saved.

Almost universally when people experience loss because of fire, flood, or other disaster what they miss the most are photographs of precious events and people. My friends were spared the loss of these treasures. Photographs help us remember special moments in our lives. When difficult circumstances rob us of our joy, memories of good times help us to persevere. Memories of good times bring us comfort when we are depressed, put a smile on our faces when we are sad and provide stability when we are confused.

✓ Describe a special memory that you treasure. How can this memory bring you comfort, joy and stability?

Mapping the Trail

The Bible is God's photo album of his character, love, forgiveness, instructions and promises. The writers of the Psalms tell us that God promises comfort, joy, stability, guidance and wisdom in his Word (Psalms 18:30-36; 37:30-31; 119:49-50, 105-107, 114).

✓ What are some verses that have been a comfort to you?

✓ What Bible stories or verses provide joy for you?

✓ How has the Bible given you stability, guidance and wisdom? Think of specific times when you have experienced these types of help from specific Bible verses.

Beginning the Ascent

When I was in the fifth grade, my Sunday school held a three-month contest for memorizing Bible verses and maintaining perfect attendance at class each Sunday. The reward for the top winners was a trip to Chicago from Grand Rapids, Michigan, where I grew up. This was a big opportunity for children who had never been away from their parents. We wanted to go to the famous city of Chicago with other kids and only a couple adults. Every Sunday we received a new set of verses to memorize. Every Monday, my sister and I began to learn these verses and commit them to memory. By the following Sunday morning, the verses were ingrained in our minds so well that we could recite them to our teacher without stumbling. The day came when the winners were announced in front of the whole church. How exciting when my name and my sister's name were called. Ten of us went to Chicago.

Little did we realize that the real reward was not the trip but the gift of God's Word hidden in our hearts forever. Many of the verses I learned long ago still come to mind when I'm in need of wisdom, comfort or joy. God's promises are the memories that sustain us through life. God's answers and principles are the guidelines for making decisions. God's plan for eternal salvation and forgiveness of sin is clearly described for us to know.

Have you ever wished you knew where the Bible said something about a certain subject? Or have you hesitated to talk about your faith because you were afraid someone might ask a question and you wouldn't know where to find the verse that gives the answer? When we have verses memorized, we can answer those questions with confidence and point others to the text for further reading.

The benefits of Scripture memory extend beyond having answers to questions. Memorizing Scripture will help you experience God's grace in a profound way because you are so close to him through his Word. You will begin to think according to his perspective on life and eternity. You will also enjoy God's life-giving help to fight against temptation to sin. Memorization roots the truth in your heart so you will recognize temptations as they rear their ugly heads. Rather than depending on hindsight for wisdom after the fact, with foresight you'll know what constitutes sin and how to say no. You will also begin to see God using you in the lives of others for his kingdom purposes. When you have God's Word in your heart and mind, God will bring people into your life who need to hear the words you know.

For many of us who have not been in the habit of memorizing Scripture, this seems like a daunting task. Yet if you think about it, your mind is filled with an abundance of memorized information, facts, trivia, numbers, words spoken to you, words you have spoken, and memories of places and moments. Your mind is the memory bank of your life. Your mind is memorizing things even when you are not aware of it. Your mind can do this. Memorizing is simply reviewing something so often it becomes well-known in your mind. Here are a few steps that will help you.

Steps in Memorizing Scripture

1. Choose a topic on which you would like to memorize a few verses. To help you find these verses, look at the back of your Bible if it has a concordance. Or borrow one from a friend or your church library. You can also purchase an exhaustive concordance at a Christian bookstore. Also, there are small books of Bible promises which contain verses on various topics.

2. Select two or three verses on this topic that are meaningful to you.

3. Read the context of the verses you have chosen so that you have the big picture of their meaning and use in the passage.

4. Write out each verse and its reference on a 3 x 5 card or a piece of note paper.

5. Begin with one verse. Read it aloud every day for three days. Include the verse reference as you read it.

6. Instead of the whole verse, start with a sentence or a phrase. Repeat this sentence or phrase from memory for the next three days, remembering to keep reading the entire verse. Read or say aloud the phrases and the reference you are learning.

7. Continue adding phrases until you have the whole verse memorized. Once you have memorized one verse, begin to memorize another.

8. As you memorize new verses, continue repeating out loud every day for six weeks each verse you have already memorized. After six weeks each verse will be yours.

> In Matthew 6:21, Jesus said, "Where your treasure is, there your heart will be also." The Bible is God's treasured gift of his Word to you. When his words are committed to memory, your heart will be close to God, your greatest treasure.

Special Hints

It is often best to have a partner for this. Someone I work with met a friend weekly for breakfast, each memorizing a new verse each week and "quizzing" one another on verses from previous weeks. The repetition and discussion of life issues related to the verses have ingrained them in his memory forever!

Take the verse cards with you in your pocket or purse.

Review the verses as you sit in your car at stoplights.

Read and review the verses as you wait in the doctor's or dentist's office or wherever you might be waiting for something.

Keep your cards in a file box in sections labeled by the topics you have chosen. Note the topic on the card in the corner. This will become a handy reference box for you to continue your review process as well as where you can place new verses you memorize through the years.

When you take a break from memorizing new verses, pick a topic and take the packet of cards from your file box with you to review the verses you have learned on that topic. (Some Christian bookstores carry sets of verses by topic.)

Gaining a Foothold

My mother is eighty-two years old. Every month she memorizes several new Bible verses, one verse at a time, phrase by phrase. When she can't sleep at night, she repeats the verses she is learning and they become her comfort in the lonely darkness. God is close to her in his Word. You will know this same comfort, joy and guidance as you begin to memorize Scripture. Begin with one verse. Enjoy the process and celebrate the victory when you have completely memorized that verse. You are on your way to treasuring God's Word in your heart and mind.

Trailmarkers

Read Psalm 119:165 together. Discuss your thoughts about this verse. What does it say will be the result of loving God's commands in his Word? Commit this verse to memory.

Teamwork

Review the verses you chose to memorize after the last session. If you have memorized your verses, say them to the group from memory. Celebrate your accomplishment together.

If you have not had a chance to begin memorizing a verse from 1 John, select one now from 1 John or from the verses listed in "Mapping the

Trail." Begin memorizing the verse of your choice.

In this fifteen minutes, memorize the first phrase of your chosen verse. Work in pairs, repeating your memorized phrases together. Congratulations! You are on your way.

 Reaching the Summit
Briefly review "Steps in Memorizing Scripture" and "Special Hints." Discuss your thoughts or questions in response.

Next Session

In this session we have considered ways to treasure God's Word through Scripture memory. In our next session we will learn how to reflect and meditate on God's Word so that it takes root in our lives.

As you continue to memorize your selected Scriptures, take five to ten minutes one day to quietly think about that verse. Let the words sink into your heart as well as your memory. This will help you begin the practice of meditation.

Close in Prayer

Pray together with your teamwork partner for a need that each of you is facing this next week.

Pray for each other in your effort to memorize your verses this next week, perhaps calling each other or meeting for coffee to share verses and encourage each other.

Session 4

Reflection & Meditation
Letting the Truth Take Root

Establishing Base Camp

In late fall of last year I joined a foundation for saving trees. In return for my membership check I received ten tree saplings. The instructions said to plant each sapling in a medium-sized container, water them regularly and in two years they would be ready to plant in the ground. As I carefully planted each one in a container with fresh soil and nutrients, I had visions of a lovely forest of trees surrounding my house. Through the Midwestern winter of snow and cold, I carefully watched each small sapling to see how they were surviving the weather. Somehow, when spring arrived, only one tree had taken root in its container. The other nine showed no signs of life.

I learned a lesson about planting trees. In order to have success, hearty roots must exist to sustain the growth of the tree. In fact, the roots are the most important part of any plant, whether it's a tree, bush or flower. Cut back the root system and the plant will not survive.

✓ Describe your personal experience planting flowers, bushes or trees. What has been your success in sustaining growth of your plant? What has contributed to failure if your plants have not survived?

Mapping the Trail

Psalm 1:3 uses the picture of a tree to symbolize our relationship with God. It tells us that if we meditate on God's Word, we will be like a growing tree that has a healthy root system gathering nutrients from the water and producing fruit at the proper time. It also indicates that because our roots are firmly planted in God's truth, we will not lose our effectiveness as fruitbearers.

Read Psalm 1:1-3.

✔ In what areas of your life do you want to grow?

✔ How do you think the Bible can help you to grow in these areas?

✔ Like a healthy tree weathering the storms of each season, how do you think the Bible can give you stability to weather the storms of your life?

Beginning the Ascent

In Psalm 1:2 the writer refers to meditating on the Scriptures day and night. Does it mean that he didn't do anything other than read the Bible all day and night? We can more fully understand the word *meditate* by its synonyms: reflect, contemplate, ponder, ruminate, think. To meditate on something is to think slowly and deeply about it, to let its truths reach so deep into the soul and mind that we assimilate the truth into our inner being, and to live out of that truth. Meditating on Scripture fills our minds and souls with God's perspective on every issue of life. God's perspective is truth. When we let God's truth take root deep in the inner recesses of our mind and soul, we will live according to his truths. It is not that the psalmist takes no action or that we are doing nothing other than sitting with the Bible on our laps. But as we reflect on the

Scriptures off and on throughout the day, we will know how to face our everyday lives with strength and confidence.

In her book *The Spiritual Art of Creative Silence,* Jeanie Miley writes, "The purpose of meditation is to encounter God, not to solve problems, enjoy fantasies, or daydream." In meditation we learn that God is bigger than our life, bigger than our problems, sorrows or frustrations. We learn that God is trustworthy and that we can entrust ourselves, our circumstances and our emotions into his hands. When meditating on Scripture we realize that we can surrender to God's infinite love, care and guidance. At first this surrender means disciplining our will because people and circumstances have fractured our foundation of trust. We have chosen independence in order to survive the disappointments we have experienced.

Meditating on the Scriptures, we discover that God is not like people. He keeps his promises. Meditation on God's truth reminds us just how much we matter to God. Over time, as we experience God's love, care and guidance again and again, surrendering to him becomes easier. Psalm 1:3 tells us that by living according to God's truths in the Scriptures, we will experience a life of purpose and influence.

By its definition, meditating takes time. It is not a quick read of a Bible passage or verse. It is a "stop and slowly think about" method of responding to Scripture. It is not a method of Bible study but a method of seeking to relate the Scripture to your own life. Meditating on Scripture is in essence a two-way conversation with God. It permits you to slow down and quiet your soul enough to ask God questions concerning what you are reading, and to hear God speak to you personally in his Word. Meditating also draws you to make a life response back to what you are reading.

How do we meditate on Scripture? It was actually in a time of sadness that I began to meditate on Scripture. My circumstances were not changing according to my prayers. Family and friends were not reaching my soul with their encouragements. I needed to understand God's perspective more fully in order to grow in my relationship with him and overcome my sadness. I decided to read the book of Psalms because the psalm writers expressed every emotion I was feeling—anger, sadness, frustration—as well as praise and thankfulness.

As I began to read, I would pause on various phrases that reflected my feelings, thoughts and circumstances. I reread the phrase and then contemplated how that phrase reflected my own life. In the Psalms I learned that *God* was the solution, not people, circumstances or wealth. God isn't fickle like people. God is stable and consistent like a rock. As I began to assimilate the truths about God in the Psalms, my sadness lifted. My circumstances didn't change but my perspective did. I could see God in my circumstances, and my love for him grew.

Meditating on the Psalms increased my understanding of who God is and how much he loves me. Since then, I have found that meditating on any passage of Scripture increases my understanding and love for God as well as my understanding and appreciation of his love for me. And you will find the same result.

Steps in Meditating on Scripture

1. Read a passage of Scripture until you come across a verse that strikes a chord in your heart. You may want to begin with a psalm. Perhaps Psalm 1, 23, 25, 32, 39, 42, 46, 62, 92, 95, 103 or 119. These are just a few of my favorites. After you complete this Bible study series, you may want to take a year and meditate on each of the psalms.

2. Once you come across a verse or set of verses that strike a chord with you, reread them. I like to underline them and write the date in the margin. I also make a note about what is going on in my life at the time of reading so that later I can remember why these verses were so meaningful on that date.

3. Picture in your mind the setting being described in this passage. For instance, many times in the Psalms, reference is made to a rock, a fortress, a stream, a light or a tree. Let your mind view the setting of the psalm. Think of the smells, the sounds and the feelings one might experience in that setting.

4. Think about what is going on in your life that makes this passage so meaningful to you.

5. Pray for God's insight into your circumstances. Let the Holy Spirit work. Repeat the Scripture passage back to God in your prayer, expressing

your own life situation.

6. Sit quietly and ask God to speak to you in this passage. As you listen, accept the truths of this passage as his message to you personally.

7. Write this verse or passage in your own words, reflecting your situation. Insert your name when appropriate. It may feel sacrilegious to rewrite a verse in the Bible. However, when we remember that God used ordinary people to write about the circumstances of their lives and how God was involved, we realize that he desires us to know and experience him in the same way in our lives. We are not rewriting the Scriptures for others, but we are letting the circumstances of the biblical writers help us to see how God is involved in our own circumstances. God is a personal God to each of his children. Rewriting a meaningful verse helps us to meditate on how God is personal in his relationship with us.

8. Respond to God in prayer, journal-writing or by reflecting your concerns. Often a verse strikes a chord in our hearts because of specific circumstances or emotional needs we are facing at the time of reading. Keeping a written journal or diary of our meditations and thoughts can be helpful. Writing helps me to keep my thoughts focused and to sort out my response to God. However, many times I don't write my thoughts. I just let my mind reflect on what the verse is saying to me. Responding to a verse is very personal. Your style of response should reflect your personality.

> Meditating on Scripture will settle your soul. It is best done when you are alone. I have found it helpful to schedule meditation time on my calendar so that the cares of life don't crowd out this solitude time of meditation and reflection.

9. Let the meaning of the verse sink deep enough in your soul that you respond with a commitment. I have found that in my meditation I always come to a moment of personal commitment in my relationship with God based on the words in the passage. This commitment may be in action and behavior, but mostly it is in releasing my situation to God because of the truth about him in this passage. At this moment I am able to surrender to God's truth in this passage and let it take root in my heart and mind. Taking time to meditate on Scripture reveals how trustworthy God really is and how much he loves and values you.

Gaining a Foothold

In times of meditation and reflection, some people prefer to have soft instrumental music playing in the background. Others prefer silence. Some people appreciate being in nature or viewing nature while meditating. Others appreciate sitting in a comfortable chair in the family room. Wherever you may be, whenever you are reading the Bible, watch for a verse that reflects God's message to you. Stop for a moment and reflect on that verse and what God is saying to you. Respond back to him with gratefulness and a deeper commitment to walk closely with him.

Trailmarkers

Sit quietly while each person reads Psalm 23:1-6. As you read, let God touch your soul with one or two verses. Reflect on this verse and how it pertains to your life. Personalize this verse by rewriting it according to your personal situation. What is your response back to God because of the truth in this verse?

Teamwork

Share with the group what verses influenced you and why. As each one feels comfortable, read the verses you rewrote. By sharing your commitments, you will encourage each other in your relationship with God, and you will understand each other at a deeper level.

Reaching the Summit

Briefly review and discuss your thoughts or questions concerning meditation. What excites you about this? What are your fears?

Next Session

In this session we have looked at how to personalize Scripture through meditation and reflection. In the next session we will look at how the Scriptures reflect God's message to us as his collective family of followers. In preparation for the next session, read Jesus' prayer for his followers in John 17.

Close in Prayer

Pray for each other concerning what each one has shared from personal reflection on Psalm 23.

Pray for your group and your personal relationships with each other.

Pray for time and wisdom for each one as you read and reflect on John 17 in preparation for the next session.

Session 5

Scripture & Community
God's Word to Us

Establishing Base Camp

A friend of mine has been in a small group with some friends for ten years. They have gone through the joys and sorrows of life together—promotions and demotions, weddings and funerals, babies and rebellious teenagers. They laugh together a lot. They cry often over the trials someone is facing. They study Scripture together and serve together in ministry opportunities at their church. They have come to know each other very well. They have even come to the place where they can say and receive tough words that indicate the need for personal transformation.

Recently some new members joined their group. They were surprised at the intensity with which some of the members expressed their feelings and frustrations. In fact, the new members were afraid to speak their own thoughts because they were different than the opinions being expressed. Although it was difficult to confront the situation, within days the new members expressed their feelings to those who had been strong in the meeting. The veteran members heard their comments, processed them personally and expressed apologies.

At their next small group gathering, the veteran members asked the group for forgiveness for their intensity and explained their own personal life struggles that were at the root of their frustrations. As a result of that experience, their group grew closer to each other because truth was spoken and heard, and because they gained deep insights into the hearts of other members. They were able to extend forgiveness and grace. The unity of their group was strengthened as well as restored. Jesus' pattern of conflict resolution found in Matthew 18:15 was followed, and it worked. Paul's words on kindness and forgiveness in Ephesians 4:32 were followed, and love was the result. God, through Scripture and through each other, had guided this small group through a potentially destructive situation. This is community at its finest.

You have now been in your small group for at least five weeks (and perhaps much more). Discuss the following questions about your feelings concerning your group:

✓ How has your personal life changed because of the learning you have experienced in the group?

✓ How has your personal life changed because of the relationships in the group?

✓ What would you like to celebrate about the group?

Mapping the Trail

Ecclesiastes 4:9-13 tells us that two are better than one for several reasons. In the beginning of time when God created the world, he gave each animal a partner. He created both male and female for the purpose of multiplying and developing the community of families. In Genesis 2:18 we read that after creating the man, God said, "It is not good for the man to be alone." He then created a partner for the man. Friendships and partnerships are a gift from God.

✓ Who are the friends in your life that have been a blessing from God to you?

✓ Who do you go to for help in discerning God's guidance for decision-making in the midst of trials?

 ## Beginning the Ascent

Throughout Scripture we see that life is meant to be experienced in community with others. In the Old Testament, community took place in families, in the synagogue and with special friends. God chose Abraham to begin a nation that God would call his people. It was through the family community of Abraham's grandson Jacob and his twelve sons that God started the nation of Israel. As this family grew in number, God further developed their community around their faith in and obedience to him. The community of friendships was also significant, as we see in the friendships of David and Jonathan (1 Samuel 18—20), Ruth and Naomi (Ruth), and Daniel and his three friends Shadrach, Meshach and Abednego (Daniel 1 and 3).

In the New Testament, community thrives in friendships and in the church. During his three years of ministry, Jesus spent most of his time with his disciples and close followers. In John 15:14-15, Jesus called them his friends. When Jesus sent his twelve disciples out on their first ministry assignment, he sent them in pairs (Mark 6:7). The apostle Paul always traveled with friends. At the end of his life, Paul asked his closest friends, Timothy, Luke and Mark, to be with him (2 Timothy 4:9, 11). In the book of Acts we read that the early Christians met together as groups in homes for fellowship and support as they discussed the teachings of the apostles and prayed for each other (Acts 2:42, 46). As the early church grew in number, God gave instructions through the letters of Paul, Peter, James and John on how his followers were to relate with each other in their communities of family, faith and friendships.

What is the type of community we are talking about? This type of community is the affinity that binds a small group of people together. It may be the affinity of family, of similar values and beliefs, of a common need or cause, or of friendship. This type of community evokes a depth of relationship that unites its members through good times and difficult times. But this type of community doesn't just happen. And the prevailing culture of our time has pulled people apart. Our interest in computer games, Internet surfing and videos has produced isolation and disconnection rather than group interaction. Family trust is broken as a result of busyness, abuse and divorce. Although we long for good friends, many of us are leery of building meaningful friendships because of past hurts and disappointments. The community experienced in my friend's group (the story at the beginning of this session) and in the biblical examples above is a desire in many of our hearts, but it will take the energy of our wills to follow guidelines God has given in his Word.

✓ The last recorded prayer of Jesus in John 17 is his longing for this type of community to be experienced by his followers. Read this prayer. As you read, look for the following requests that Jesus prayed.

1. For Jesus and the Father to be glorified (vv. 1, 5)

2. For eternal life for his followers who have believed his words (vv. 2-3, 6-8, 24)

3. For unity in faith with the Father, Jesus and each other (vv. 11, 21-22)

4. For Jesus' joy to be full in their hearts (v. 13)

5. For the Father to keep them from the evil one (v. 15)

6. For the Father to set his followers apart in the truth of his word (v. 17)

7. For his followers to experience the love of the Father to the Son (v. 26)

8. That the result might be that the world will know the truth about God the Father and Son (vv. 21, 23)

Notice the flow of this prayer. Jesus was concerned about the unity of believers with the Father, himself and each other. A friendship with Jesus is the beginning of this type of community. In John 13:35 Jesus tells us that the world will know we are his followers by the love we have for each other. In his prayer in John 17, we also see that unity between believers will bring glory to God in the eyes of the *world,* meaning those who do not follow after

> "Genuine communion with God translates into active participation in the building of community. It is impossible to love God without loving our neighbor since, in the actual practice of love, our service to God can only find expression in our service to others." (Gilbert Bilezikian, *Community 101*)

Jesus. The type of community described above is so unusual it will be a testimony to our personal worlds that God is love.

After unity, Jesus prayed for us to experience his joy. Joy flows out of a pure love relationship with him. However, because we are in this world where the evil one seeks to destroy us, our unity and our joy, Jesus prays that we will be protected from that destruction. As a result of our relationship with God, our unity with each other and the joy of Jesus in our hearts, Jesus prays that our lives will be useful for his glory in the world. In community with Jesus and each other we find purpose for living.

The New Testament reveals God's guidelines on how to develop and maintain this unity with him and each other. God's purposes for us are to love him and love each other. Jesus said the two greatest commandments are to love God and each other (Matthew 22:36-40). Hebrews 10:24-25 encourages us to meet together in our churches and to stimulate each other to love and kind deeds. God's word to us is to be in community together with him and with each other.

Trailmarkers

Read Galatians 5:22—6:2, 9-10. Reread each verse and discuss how each verse depicts your group and how your group can grow in application of each verse.

Gaining a Foothold

Biblical community, unity of spirit and mind with others expressed in love, takes a willingness to be vulnerable, teachable and honest about our feelings. When we live out of our value to God, who tells us in Scripture how much he loves each of us, we can value others enough to share our inner thoughts and to appreciate their inner thoughts. Romans 8:16 tells us that God the Holy Spirit communicates with our spirit about his love for and value of us, assuring us that we are his children. But often the voices of our world speak more loudly in our ears, telling us that we have no value. Listening to the Spirit's voice in our heart instead of the human voices in our head will give us the confidence to build loving and trusting community with others.

Teamwork

Affirm the community of your group in one of the two ways that follow.

✓ Have each person in the group choose one characteristic listed in the verses above that fits the person sitting to his or her left. As a group, go around the circle sharing each affirmation while all the group listens.

✓ Choose a chair in the room as a "hot seat." Have each person in the group take a turn sitting on the hot seat. Every member of the group then affirms that person concerning how he or she has demonstrated the characteristics listed in these verses. Because of limited time, each person should only express one of the characteristics about the person in the hot seat so that everyone has an opportunity to share their affirmations.

Reaching the Summit

The affirmations you have just shared have brought you to a summit in the life of your group. Where else in life will you receive so much love and affirmation? Take a few minutes to thank each other for the words of encouragement you have received.

Next Session

The next session is a summary of these five sessions. In preparation for your group time, it will be most helpful if each person in your group completes the materials in session six.

Close in Prayer

Pray for each group member as they face the week ahead that the affirmations of this session will ring in their head and heart.

Pray for every group member that God will touch each heart this week with his affirmation.

Session 6

Putting It All Together

Establishing Base Camp

Some years ago, my sister and I decided we would like to learn how to downhill snow ski. We went to a ski shop to buy the necessary jackets, gloves and socks. We got fitted with rental skis and boots, and we bought a rack to put the skis on the top of the car. We were looking good. Thinking we had everything we needed to master the slopes, we set out to meet our instructor.

First lesson: how to put the boots and skis on and "walk" with these long narrow extensions on our feet and with our ankles barely able to flex. Next lesson: how to get up after losing our balance as we walked. After a few more lessons on how to navigate the ski lifts, do the "snow-plow," and turn from side-to-side, we were ready to put together all we had learned and attempt the intermediate hill. The more adept we became at putting together all the skills that we had learned in our lessons, the more confident we were to go out on our own without the instructor. Skiing became one of the highlights of winter.

✔ Think of an experience in your life when you have had to employ varied skills or learning in order to enjoy the experience to its fullest. Perhaps it was learning how to ride your first bike, or how to drive the car, or water ski, or accomplish some task at work. Describe the various skills necessary for you to enjoy your experience. Explain how it felt when you put all the skills together and accomplished what you were trying to do. Explain how you felt in the process of learning the skills before you experienced the end result.

Mapping the Trail

As we have learned in this study guide, there are multiple styles and skills available for reading, studying and enjoying the Bible, God's Word to us. Each style by itself is rewarding and enjoyable. However when we employ all these styles in our relationship with God, Bible reading will be not only a time of learning about God but a time when we worship God as well.

Just as each of us best learns in different ways, so also we enjoy different styles of reading the Bible and relating to God. Describe how you like to relate to God and his Word.

✓ Which styles have you enjoyed? Why?

✓ Which style have you not enjoyed? Why?

✓ Which style do you enjoy using the most? Why?

Beginning the Ascent

Before we begin to put all the Bible-reading styles together, let's do a quick review. Look back at each session and review your responses. Talk about what you like in each style and about any frustrations or confusion you have about each style.

Devotional Reading—God's Word to Me. "Reading the Bible devotion-ally is to read it as a lover reads a love letter—with the heart, with an open mind and with the attitude of a learner" (session one). Reading the Bible devotionally will reveal God's heart of love for you. Although his Word is universal to all, God speaks to each of us individually in his Word. It is in times of quiet, slow, devotional reading, with a heart open to listen to God, that we hear his individual message of love to us, which meets our unique need. Review the steps in "How to Read Devotionally" and the "Treasures to Look For in Devotional Reading."

A Well-Ordered Heart—My Response to God. In the Bible we find that God receives our love through our community with him in prayer and through our obedience to his commandments. Although earthly parents and authority figures fail us by not consistently showing their love, God is the ideal parent who never fails to demonstrate his love for each of us. His love is working for our good in the midst of a world that often sabotages our good. "A well-ordered heart is a heart at peace with God and self" (pullout quote, session two).

Scripture Memory—Treasuring God's Word. "Memorizing is simply reviewing something so often it becomes well-known in your mind" (session three). Memorizing Scripture takes the discipline to review verses until they are known in your mind. The benefits of Scripture memory include knowing where to find needed verses, experiencing God's grace in new ways, thinking according to God's perspective, recognizing sin as it creeps up on us, and seeing God use you in the lives of others for his purposes. Review the "Steps in Memorizing Scripture" and the "Special Hints."

Reflection and Meditation—Letting the Truth Take Root. "Meditating on Scripture is in essence a two-way conversation with God. It permits you to slow down and quiet your soul enough to ask God questions con-cerning what you are reading, and to hear God speak to you personally in his Word" (session four). Taking time to slowly read and think about the Scriptures creates a setting for you to ponder and respond to what you are reading. The end result will be that the truth of what you are reading will take root deep in your soul. Out of that truth you will make wise deci-sions and right choices in your daily life. Review the "Steps in Meditating on Scripture."

Scripture & Community—God's Word to Us. "God's purposes for us are to love him and love each other. . . . God's word to us is to be in community together with him and with each other" (session five). God has given us guidelines in his Word on how to live with each other and strengthen our

> The Bible is about God. It was written to reveal his glory. When we read and respond to the truths in the Bible, we are responding to and honoring God.

relationships. According to John 1:12, believers in Jesus as personal Savior, Lord and friend are the family of God. His family is called a body in Romans 12, where we find guidelines on how members of this body are to function with each other.

Scripture Reading and Response Exercise

Richard Foster aptly says in *Prayer:* "So many passages of Scripture provide a touchstone for meditative prayer: 'Be still and know that I am God'; 'Abide in my love'; 'I am the good shepherd'; 'Rejoice in the Lord always.' In each case we are seeking to discover God near us and are longing to encounter his presence."

✓ Read Romans 12 through two times devotionally, allowing it to sink in. Record the verses that stand out to you. Ask God to reveal his personal message to you.

✓ Write out your commitment to obey his communication. Verses 9-21 have many commands to consider. Find one or two that require particular attention. Journal your thoughts as you reflect and respond back to God.

✓ Choose a verse or two that you want to memorize. Romans 12:1-2 is very powerful if you need some help choosing.

✓ Choose a passage, verse or word to meditate on.

✓ Share with the group what God is teaching you. Let this chapter speak to your heart in relationship to God's love for you and his power working through you to impact your world.

Gaining a Foothold

There are days when my Bible reading seems dry, maybe because of the passage I'm reading that day, or because of what else is going on in my life, or just because my mind can't focus on the verses I'm reading. This will happen for you too. It's normal.

The key is not to give up reading. Try a different style of reading. Listen to some praise and worship music first. Ask God to enter your mind and to guide your thoughts in his direction. When the angels announced the birth of Jesus to the shepherds, they said they had news of a great joy. Jesus was that joy (Luke 2:10-11). He is still our joy. The more we read, meditate on, memorize and internalize the Scriptures, the more we will find our joy in Jesus and the more we will desire to respond to him with our lives.

Trailmarkers

Read Romans 12:1-21. Talk about which verses were especially meaningful to you in your preparation. Encourage each one to recite the verse memorized and explain why he or she chose that verse to memorize.

Teamwork

From your reading in this chapter of the various styles this past week, share with your group your thoughts and feelings about your relationship with God. If your group is larger than five people, it may be best to work in smaller groups so that everyone has the opportunity to share and hear from others.

Reaching the Summit

Congratulations! You have put it all together by completing this study guide. You have learned and experienced several styles for reading your Bible. You have gained deeper insights into God and your relationship with him. You have grown in your relationship with the other members of your small group. You have applied the truths to your life that you have read.

✓ What have you learned about yourself as you participated in this study?

✓ What have you learned about God?

✓ What have you learned about each other?

Next Session

Plan a party to celebrate your completion of this study guide. Discuss together your plans for what materials to study next.

Close in Prayer

Pray for all group members as they face the week ahead that the joy of Jesus will fill each heart.

Pray for specific concerns each group member is facing that God will give his wisdom, insight and comfort where needed.

Leader's Notes

Few ventures are more defining than leading a group that produces changed lives and sharper minds for the cause of Christ. At Willow Creek we have seen small groups transform our church, offer deeper levels of biblical community and provide an environment where truth can be understood and discussed with enthusiasm. So we have focused on a group-based study rather than a classroom-lecture format or individual study (though these studies can profitably be used in both settings with minor adaptations).

Each method of learning has its strengths; each has its weaknesses. In personal study one can spend as little or as much time as desired on an issue and can focus specifically on personal needs and goals. The downside: there is no accountability to others, no one to challenge thoughts or assumptions, no one to provide support when life comes tumbling down around you. The classroom is ideal for proclaiming truth to many at one time and for having questions answered by those with expertise or knowledge in a subject area. But the pace of the class depends largely on the teacher, and there is limited time to engage in the discussion of personal issues. The small group is optimal for life-on-life encouragement, prayer and challenge. And it provides a place where learning is enhanced through the disciplines of biblical community. But small groups are usually not taught by content experts and cannot focus solely on one person's needs.

Our hope is that you will be able to use this curriculum in a way that draws from the best of all three methods. Using the small group as a central gathering place, personal preparation and study will allow you to focus on your own learning and growth goals. The small group activity will provide you with an engaging environment for refining your understanding and gaining perspective into the lives and needs of others. And perhaps by inviting a knowledgeable outsider to the group (or a cluster of small groups at a Saturday seminar, for example) you could gain the benefits of solid teaching in a given subject area. In any case your devotion to

Christ, your commitment to your local church and your obedience to the Word of God are of utmost importance to us. Our desire is to see you "grow in the grace and knowledge of the Lord Jesus Christ."

Leadership Tips

Here are some basic guidelines for leaders. For more extensive leadership support and training we recommend that you consult *The Willow Creek Guide to Leading Lifechanging Small Groups,* where you will find many suggestions for leading creative groups.

Using the leader's notes. The questions in the study will not be repeated in the leader's notes. Instead, we have provided comments, clarifications, additional information, leadership tips or group exercises. These will help you guide the discussion and keep the meeting on track.

Shared leadership. When leading a small group remember that your role is to guide the discussion and help draw people into the group process. Don't try to be the expert for everything. Seek to involve others in the leadership process and activities of group life (hosting meetings, leading prayer, serving one another, leading parts of the discussion and so forth).

Preparation. Your work between meetings will determine group effectiveness during meetings. Faithful preparation does not mean that you will control the meeting or that it will move exactly as you planned. Rather, it provides you with a guiding sense of the desired outcomes of the time together so that you can gauge the pace of the meeting and make adjustments along the way. Above all, make sure you are clear about the overall goal of the meeting. Then, even if you get appropriately sidetracked dealing with a personal concern or a discussion of related issues, you can graciously help the group refocus on the goal of the meeting. Also, preparation will allow you to observe how others are engaging with the material. *You should complete the study* before coming to the meeting. You can participate in the group activities at the meeting, but take time to become personally acquainted with the material in case you need to alter the schedule or amount of time on each section.

Purpose. The series is designed to help people understand the Word and be confident in their ability to read, study and live its lifechanging truths. Bible 101 is not designed for a group whose primary goal is caregiving or support. That does not mean you will avoid caring for each other, praying for needs or supporting one another through personal crises. It simply means that the *entire* focus of the group is not for these purposes. At the same time, the content should never take precedence over the process of transformation. There will be appropriate times to set the curriculum aside and pray. Or you may want to spend an evening having fun together. Remember, Jesus did not say, "Go therefore into all the world and complete the curriculum." Our focus is to make disciples. The curriculum is a tool, not a master. Use it consistently and with discernment, and your group will be well-served. But be clear about the primary focus of the group as you gather, and remind people every few weeks about the core purpose so that the group does not drift. So even though this is designed for six meetings per study guide, you might take longer if you have a meeting that focuses entirely on prayer or service.

Length of Meeting. We assume that you have about seventy to ninety minutes for this meeting, including prayer and some social time. If you have more or less time, adjust accordingly, especially if you have a task-based group. In that case, since you must complete the task (working on a ministry team or serving your church in some way), you will have to be selective in what you cover unless you can devote at least one hour to the meeting. In the format described below, feel free to play with the time allowed for "Beginning the Ascent," "Trailmarkers" and "Teamwork." We have given general guidelines for time to spend on each section. But depending on the size of group (we recommend about eight members), familiarity with the Bible and other group dynamics, you will have to make adjustments. After a few meetings you should have a good idea of what it will take to accomplish your goals.

Format. We have provided you with a general format. But feel free to provide some creativity or a fresh approach. You can begin with prayer, for example, or skip the "Establishing Base Camp" group opener and dive right into the study. We recommend that you follow the format closely early in the group process. As your group and your leadership skills mature and progress, you should feel increasing freedom to bring your creativity and experience to the meeting format. Here is the framework for the format in each of the guides in this series.

 Establishing Base Camp

This orients people to the theme of the meeting and usually involves a group opener or icebreaker. Though not always directly related to the content, it will move people toward the direction for the session. A base camp is the starting point for any mountain journey.

 Mapping the Trail

In this component we get clear about where we will go during the meeting. It provides an overview without giving away too much and removing curiosity.

 Beginning the Ascent

This is the main portion of the meeting: the climb toward the goal. It is the teaching and discussion portion of the meeting. Here you will find questions and explanatory notes. You will usually find the following two components included.

Pullouts. These provide additional detail, clarification or insight into content or questions that may arise in the participants' minds during the session.

Charts/Maps. Visual learners need more than words on a page. Charts, maps and other visuals combined with the content provide a brief, concise summary of the information and how it relates.

Gaining a Foothold
Along the trail people can drift off course or slip up in their understanding. These footholds are provided for bringing them into focus on core issues and content.

 Trailmarkers
These are key biblical passages or concepts that guide our journey. Participants will be encouraged to memorize or reflect on them for personal growth and for the central biblical basis behind the teaching.

 Teamwork
This is a group project, task or activity that builds a sense of community and shared understanding. It will be different for each study guide and for each lesson, depending on the author's design and the purpose of the content covered.

 Reaching the Summit
This is the end of the content discussion, allowing members to look back on what they have learned and capture it in a brief statement or idea. This "view from the top" will help them once again focus on the big picture after spending some time on the details.

Balancing caregiving and study/discussion. One of the most difficult things to do in a group, as I alluded to above, is balancing the tension between providing pastoral and mutual care to members and getting through the material. I have been in small groups where needs were ignored to get the work done, and I have been in groups where personal needs were the driving force of the group to the degree that the truth of the Word was rarely discussed. These guides are unique because they are designed to train and teach processes that must take place in order to achieve its purpose. But the group would fail miserably if someone came to a meeting and said, "I was laid off today from my job," and the group said a two-minute prayer and then opened their curriculum. So what do you do? Here are some guidelines.

1. People are the most important component of the group. They have real needs. Communicate your love and concern for people, even if they don't always get all the work done or get sidetracked.

2. When people disclose hurts or problems, address each disclosure with empathy and prayer. If you think more time should be devoted to someone, set aside time at the end of the meeting, inviting members to stay for additional prayer or to console the person. Cut the meeting short by ten minutes to accomplish this. Or deal with it right away for ten to fifteen minutes, take a short break, then head into the study.

3. Follow up with people. Even if you can't devote large portions of the meeting time to caregiving, you and others from the group can provide this between meetings over the phone or in other settings. Also learn to leverage your time. For example, if your meeting begins at 7:00 p.m., ask the member in need and perhaps one or two others from the group to come at 6:30 p.m. for sharing and prayer. A person will feel loved, your group will share in the caregiving, and it is not another evening out for people.

4. Assign prayer partners or groups of three to be little communities within the group. Over the phone or in occasional meetings outside the group (before church and so on) they could connect and check in on how life is going.

5. For serious situations, solicit help from others, including pastors or other staff at church. Do not go it alone. Set boundaries for people with serious care needs, letting them know that the group can devote some but not substantial meeting time to support them. "We all know that Dave is burdened by his son's recent illness, so I'd like to spend the first ten minutes tonight to lift him up in prayer and commit to support Dave through this season. Then, after our meeting I'd like us to discuss any specific needs you (Dave) might have over the next two to three weeks (such as meals, help with house chores, etc.) and do what we can to help you meet those needs." Something to that effect can keep the group on track but still provide a place to express compassion.

Take time to look at the entire series if you have chosen only one of the guides. Though each can be used as a stand-alone study, there is much to benefit from in the other guides because each covers material essential for a complete overview of how to study and understand the Bible. We designed the guides in series form so that you can complete them in about a year if you meet weekly, even if you take a week off after finishing each guide.

A Word About Leadership

One of your key functions as a small group leader is to be a cheerleader—someone who seeks out signs of spiritual progress in others and makes some noise about it. What have you seen God doing in your group members' lives as a result of this study? Don't assume they've seen that progress—and definitely don't assume they are beyond needing simple words of encouragement. Find ways to point out to people the growth you've seen. Let them know it's happening, and that it's noticeable to you and others.

There aren't a whole lot of places in this world where people's spiritual progress is going to be recognized and celebrated. After all, wouldn't you like to hear someone say something like that to you? Your group members feel the same way. You have the power to make a profound impact through a sincere, insightful remark.

Be aware also that some groups get sidetracked by a difficult member or situation that hasn't been confronted. And some individuals could be making significant progress, but they just need a nudge. "Encouragement" is not about just saying "nice" things; it's about offering *words that urge.* It's about giving courage (en-*courage*-ment) to those who lack it.

So leaders, take a risk. Say what needs to be said to encourage your members as they grow in their knowledge of the Bible. Help them not just amass more information, but move toward the goal of becoming fully devoted followers of Jesus Christ. Go ahead; make their day!

Session 1. Devotional Reading.
Introduce the Session (1 min.) Go over the purpose and the goal.

Purpose: This session is designed to explain how to read the Bible devotionally. This style of reading will increase our love for God and his message to us.

Goal: To make you confident in reading the Bible devotionally.

Some people feel comfortable reading the Bible devotionally and letting it speak to them. Others are action people who like to read the Bible fast so they can get on to the next activity of the day. Some people are afraid to read the Bible devotionally because they are not sure how to ponder over what they read. Help your group to see the benefits of reading the Bible devotionally, watching for what God is saying to each one individually. We want to foster a desire to read the Bible devotionally and a confidence in doing this.

Establishing Base Camp (10 min.) Discuss this question together, giving each group member time to recall their thoughts about a letter from someone important in their life. If someone has never received this kind of a letter, help him or her to think about a response. It will be helpful for you to begin this discussion with a story of your own concerning a letter you have received and your thoughts about it.

Mapping the Trail (10 min.) Begin this time with a brief discussion concerning what your group members think about the Bible. Do they think of it as a love letter or as a book of rules? Do they enjoy reading it or do they read it out of a sense of duty? Let each group member answer the questions listed in this section. If your group is larger than six, you may want to divide into smaller groups or into partners so that each person has the opportunity to answer these questions. By answering these questions, members will look into their own habits of Bible reading as well as into their own heart concerning their personal feelings about reading the Bible. Listening to each other's Bible reading habits will help you all to understand each other better as you progress in this study.

🐾 **Beginning the Ascent (30 min.)** Read this section together. Before reading the guidelines and "Treasures to Look For" sections, discuss the following:

☐ Why it is important to God that we read the Bible?

☐ What are the thoughts of your group members concerning reading the Bible devotionally? Discuss each one's perception of this method of reading the Bible.

Read and discuss the guidelines for reading the Bible devotionally. Ask your group members to describe how to read with the heart as well as the mind. Does anyone have any concerns or questions about these guidelines?

Read Psalm 23 following these guidelines. The Psalms are wonderful texts for reading devotionally. This psalm is familiar and could easily be read too quickly— without gleaning all that God has in it for each individual. Help your group practice reading slowly and soaking in the truths of each verse.

☐ Read verse 1 and then pause. Sit quietly for one minute so each one can hear God's message to him or her concerning their life circumstances right now.

☐ Suggest that group members write down their thoughts and feelings. You may want to provide a special journal for each group member at this time. This can be a spiral notebook or a cloth-covered journal. Some may want to only keep track of their personal feelings and thoughts. Some may choose to keep track of the comments from the other group members. Either way is fine. It is important to begin to let God speak to us through his Word. Sometimes it is also helpful to watch how God speaks to others as a way of learning to listen to God and as a matter for prayer requests.

☐ After this pause, read verse 2 and pause again for your group members to reflect on this verse.

☐ Continue this process through the six verses without having members share their thoughts or feelings.

☐ After you have finished reading this psalm devotionally, ask if anyone would like to discuss their writings. Respect those who choose not to participate. This will help them feel safe to truly hear from God. In the future they may share when they feel ready.

Read and discuss the list of "Treasures to Look for in Devotional Reading." Read through Psalm 23 once again. This time look for the suggestions listed in this section. Ask the group after each verse what they see in that verse as a special message, a promise, a command, a timeless principle or a personal application.

Gaining a Foothold (5 min.) Read this to your group. Briefly discuss the quote from E. Stanley Jones. Help your group appreciate how important reading the Bible is if they want to grow in their relationship with God. Discuss the difference between reading, studying and devotionally reading the Bible. This would be a good time to have each member schedule an "appointment" on their calendar to devotionally read the Bible during this next week. The purpose of this study is not to make legalistic rules concerning reading the Bible, but to challenge each one toward deeper levels of growth and love for God.

Trailmarkers (10 min.) This can be done all together or in three smaller groups, with each one taking one of the passages. After five or six minutes come back together and talk about the findings of each group.

Teamwork (15 min.) This psalm is one of my personal favorites because it reveals so much about God and his love for us. Because of the length of this psalm, it may be helpful for you to once again divide your group into smaller groups and assign specific verses to each group. Follow the steps in "Beginning the Ascent."

Reaching the Summit (5 min.) Read this section together. Let group members express their personal thoughts about setting time aside for devotional reading. Discuss how these guidelines for devotional reading require no agenda but rather openness for God to speak.

Next Session (5 min.) Encourage the members of your group to read 1 John. There are five chapters in this letter. Each chapter has references concerning our response to God's message. It will be helpful if each group member reads all five chapters before your next meeting. However, because of the busyness of life, it may be more practical for each member to take a different chapter and come prepared to share what they learned from that chapter with the group next time.

Close in Prayer (10 min.) If your group is new, you may want to lead in a prayer of thankfulness for God's love for each one in your group. Pray for them by name. If your group has been together for a while, ask them to form prayer partners with one other person to pray for each other as they face the coming week and as they commit to devotionally reading 1 John.

Session 2. A Well-Ordered Heart.
Introduce the Session (1 min.) Go over the purpose and the goal.

Purpose: This session is designed to explain God's way of receiving our love. In this session we will consider how to read the Bible as God's message to us and how to respond back to him.

Goal: To make you confident in responding to God's love revealed in the Bible.

Some people respond to God's love with joy and full acceptance. Others are not able to respond in this way because they have not experienced unconditional love from authority figures in their lives. Explain to the group that this is a safe place for them to express doubts and hurts that might be hindering them from receiving or responding to God's love. You will have the opportunity to discuss these issues later in this session under "Mapping the Trail."

Establishing Base Camp (10 min.) Discuss these questions, giving each group member time to reflect on each scenario. You might challenge them with a question like: "Describe a time you expressed love and the other person didn't receive your expression of love as you intended. How did you feel?" The five love languages are listed as a way to organize people's thoughts.

Mapping the Trail (10 min.) Discuss these questions. Many people have a hard time seeing God's love for them personally. They might be convinced that God loves the world. Certainly he loves others more than he loves them. For people who bear the scars of wounds inflicted by someone they love (or by the tough circumstances of life), it is often difficult to see God's love expressed for them personally. You may want to discuss these questions in smaller groups of two to four people so everyone feels safe and has time to fully answer. It will be wise for all your group members to listen attentively and to join in the emotions of the one speaking but not to offer advice at this time of how to see God's love. Take more than the ten minutes if you need it.

Beginning the Ascent (30 min.) If your group members have not read this section before your meeting, read it now together. The main thoughts for you to point out and discuss as a group include:

□ Jesus' relationship with God the Father and how he expressed his love to the Father.

□ The fact that God calls himself our Father and how your group members react to this name. Depending on the model of their own fathers, each one may have a different perspective on God as Father. Often our relationship with God is a mirror image of our relationship with our own fathers. It is helpful for people to see this correlation.

□ Spending time with God in prayer and obeying his commandments. What does this look like for each of your group members? How do they feel about these as being God's love language? If they feel God's love language is something different, be sure they can give a biblical reference for their findings. God's love language is not a mystery. He has clearly revealed his desires to us, so it is important for us to respond to him accordingly. Any references that reveal his desired response from us will be helpful. An opinion based on a nonbiblical rationale is not God's preferred response. That is why it is important for opinions to be based on Scripture references. Obedience is often a hard concept to accept, and so people will try to figure out many other solutions.

☐ A well-ordered heart. What does this look like for each member in your group? Talk about this together using the picture given in the pullout section.

Gaining a Foothold (5 min.) Read this to your group. Also read 1 Samuel 8 to give the background of when Israel asked for a human king. Take time to discuss how we give control of our lives to others. You may want to ask each group member who they feel has power over their lives. Once again, this is a very sensitive issue. It will be important for you to help your group understand how much God wants to rule and lead in their lives for their personal good. This may be a time when someone wants to pray for God to be the King of his or her life. Be open to how the Holy Spirit may be moving in the hearts of your people. Pray in advance that he will work and that you will know how to respond at the time of your session.

Trailmarkers (10 min.) This can be done together or in smaller groups. In this session we are concentrating on God's love language from us, but in these passages we read his love language to us. You may want to ask your members to express what they feel is the love language that they would like to receive from God. If it is different than wisdom and guidance, ask if anyone knows a reference that describes God's love in this preferred way. God knows each individual according to the intimate details of our hearts. He is too creative to show love in only one or two ways. These two references are used here because many people are looking for wisdom and guidance in our culture and world.

Teamwork (15 min.) You can break into pairs (as suggested in the study) or ask four different members of your group to read one of these chapters out loud to the group. (Try to choose people who will not feel awkward reading publicly; if you are not sure, ask for four volunteers rather than assigning this reading.) Ask someone to keep track of the verses and ways God receives our love.

Discuss the lists together. You may want to discuss each chapter after it has been read, or you may want to take all four chapters as a whole and discuss the thoughts as a whole. This is the time to bring home the application of obedience as our response to God's love. This may take more than the fifteen minutes allotted.

Reaching the Summit (5 min.) This is a time of summary. You may want to briefly redefine and explain these concepts, or you may ask various group members to express what was meaningful to them individually as they went through this session.

Next Session (5 min.) Encourage the members of your group to reread 1 John and choose a passage that touches their heart. If they want to begin memorizing, that's great. However, in the next session we will talk about why and how to memorize Scripture.

Close in Prayer (10 min.) Depending on time, you may want to pray for your group or you may want the members to pray for each other in their discussion partnerships. Because of the personal nature of your discussions, be sure to pray for each person specifically.

Session 3. Scripture Memory.
Introduce the Session (1 min.) Go over the purpose and the goal for the session.

Purpose: This session is designed to guide you in memorizing Scripture verses and passages so that God's Word is a resource to you for comfort, wisdom and direction in all the various situations of life.

Goal: To build your confidence in memorizing Bible verses.

Many people avoid memorizing Bible verses because they fear they won't be able to do it or because they don't think they have time. In this session we will learn some helpful hints toward memorizing Scripture that will not overwhelm the beginner. And these hints will encourage someone who is comfortable with Scripture memory in their continued efforts. If you as the leader struggle with memorizing verses, let your group members know. Encourage them that you will be learning how to do this with them. If this is not a struggle for you, share with your members the benefits you have experienced as a result of having memorized Bible verses.

 Establishing Base Camp (10 min.) If you prepare far enough ahead, ask each group member to bring a photo that they treasure. Or if you could not contact them in time, simply show your group some photos that you treasure. Explain how these photos touch your emotions and memory. Ask each one to share how the memory and photograph of a good or bad time they have had makes them feel.

Mapping the Trail (10 min.) Talk about God's Word as his photo album, describing his character, his heart and his home. Read the passages listed and ask your group members to each describe one "photo" in God's Word that is a treasure to them. Use the questions provided as a springboard for this discussion.

Beginning the Ascent (30 min.) If your group members have not read this section before your gathering, read it now. Discuss the following points.

☐ Has anyone had an experience with memorizing Scripture in the past? How did it go? Was it a positive experience or a negative one? Why?

☐ Has anyone experienced the hesitation of sharing the faith because he or she felt inadequate to answer questions? Let the person explain a time when this happened and how it felt.

☐ Has anyone experienced the frustration of not knowing or remembering where the Bible gives an answer to someone's question? Who has made the comment, "Somewhere in the Bible it says . . ."?

☐ What do your group members believe the benefits of Scripture memory are for thinking according to God's perspective, resisting temptations to sin and being used by God in the lives of other people?

☐ What things are easily memorized by your group members, such as telephone numbers, trivia facts and people's names? Discuss why these things are easy to memorize and why Bible verses might not be so easy to memorize.

Read through "Steps in Memorizing Scripture." When you read straight through this list, it may seem overwhelming. Encourage your group that you will take these steps one by one when you begin to memorize a verse together later in the lesson.

Read through the special hints. It will be helpful if you have a file box with 3 x 5 cards and separating index cards in it. Label some of the index cards with topics on which you want to memorize verses. Ask your group what categories or topics they would like to choose for memorizing verses. Show them how to set up their own personal file box and how to use it according to the special hints.

Trailmarkers (10 min.) This can be done together or in smaller groups. It is important to focus on a love of God's commands—his teaching. The result of this is peace and confidence. Smaller groups or partnerships will allow each member of your group to have an opportunity to share and to practice memorizing the verse.

Teamwork (15 min.) If anyone has chosen or has memorized a verse from 1 John, let them say it to the group. Celebrate their choice and their work.

To walk through the steps listed in "Beginning the Ascent," choose a verse that you will all begin to memorize together at this time, or let your group members work as partners on a verse of their choice. Read the context of the verse. Have each member write out the verse on a 3 x 5 card. Ask three people to read the verse and its reference out loud to the group. Begin with the first phrase. Repeat it three times without looking at the text. Continue memorizing this verse together phrase by phrase, repeating each phrase three times as well as the previous phrases that you have already learned. Have fun together as you memorize this verse. If mistakes are made along the way, laugh and start again. Help your group members see how much fun Scripture memory can be. Celebrate in a creative way that you have all memorized this verse.

Reaching the Summit (5 min.) In this summary time, ask your group members what they think about each step of the process. Many times we want to take shortcuts in memory work. Encourage your group not to take shortcuts this week but to follow each of these steps. They will be excited when you meet next time to have memorized at least one more verse.

Next Session (5 min.) Encourage your group members to take five to ten minutes some day before your next meeting to quietly think about the verse they are memorizing, reflecting on the words, letting the meaning of those words reach into the deepest part of their hearts and minds.

Close in Prayer (10 min.) Depending on time, you may want to pray for your group or you may want the members to pray for each other in partnerships. Be sure each group member is prayed for individually. Praying for each other will bond your group together.

Session 4. Reflection & Meditation.
Introduce the Session (1 min.) Go over the purpose and goal with the group.

Purpose: To understand how to meditate on the Word of God so that we know the truth and how to live in our society according to the truth.

Goal: To build our understanding and confidence in meditating on Bible verses.

Caution: Many people avoid meditating on Scripture because of their preconceived ideas of meditation. Help your small group members to understand that meditating on Scripture is not emptying their minds. Such techniques of "emptying oneself" are taught by Eastern mystics or New Age practitioners but are not found in the Bible. Biblical meditation is *filling* the mind with a deeper awareness of God's truth.

Others avoid meditating on Scripture because of the time it takes to be quiet and to think slowly about the Scripture and their lives. Still others avoid meditating on Scripture because they have never been taught how to do this or because they have never thought about it.

You may want to take a few minutes up front in your time together to discuss any experiences, feelings or fears your group members have about this type of exercise. Help them understand that meditating on the Scriptures will enhance their growth in their relationship with God. Stop here and pray for the group as you continue on into this session.

 Establishing Base Camp (10 min.) Discuss the questions listed. Help your group see the importance of the root system and also the importance of soft ground for the roots to be able to grow and sustain the plant.

Mapping the Trail (10 min.) Read Psalm 1:1-3 aloud. You may read it, have a group member read it or read it all together. If people are using different versions of the Bible, it will be best to have one person read it at a time. However, you may want to have the different translations read so everyone can hear the differences.

Discuss the questions listed in this section. If your group is large, it might be wise to form smaller groups so each person can share their answers to these questions.

Beginning the Ascent (30 min.) Read this section as a group and, after each paragraph, discuss any questions or comments members have. Use the thoughts in each paragraph to help dispel the fears or concerns your group members expressed at the beginning of this meeting.

After you read through "Steps in Meditating on Scripture," take one of your favorite passages of Scripture and walk through each step together. Since this may be the first time some of your group members have thought this deeply about Scripture, they may not be ready to make a commitment as suggested in step nine. That's okay. The main thing about this section is that they learn how meaningful this type of Bible reading is. Help your group members to grasp what is being asked in each step. This may take some time to explain. It may also be helpful if you or someone in the group models each step using the passage you have chosen so that everyone understands.

Refer to the pullout. Talk about when each group member could schedule some time to meditate in the coming weeks before your next group meeting.

Refer to the "Gaining a Foothold" section. Discuss each one's style of meeting with God.

Trailmarkers (10 min.) Since this is a very familiar psalm, it will be comfortable for those who are still unsure of this style of reading. If you are meeting in a home, it will be helpful if your group members can spread out into different rooms so they do not get distracted by each other. If this is not possible, encourage them to work individually, not focusing on other group members.

Help your group not to get caught on verses they might not understand but to intentionally watch for a verse that expresses the need or desire of their heart. Tell them in advance that you will let them know when seven minutes have passed so they can have enough time to think about their response back to God.

Sometimes the rewriting step is difficult for people. If this is the case for some of your group members, encourage them to think about how this verse relates to their personal situation and to talk to God in silent prayer about their thoughts.

 Teamwork (15 min.) If your group is larger than five or six, you may want to form two or more groups so that each one can share his or her thoughts and response. If your group has four or fewer people, do this section together as a group. Let each person share his or her thoughts, writing and response without interruption by anyone else in the group. As the leader, affirm all in what they have said. After each one has shared, ask the member sitting on the right of that person to pray for him or her reflecting what has been shared.

 Reaching the Summit (5 min.) In this summary time, ask your group members how they felt about each step as you went through Psalm 23. The goal in this section is that each one understands every step. However, this will also be a time when you can once again affirm the importance of meditating on Scripture passages and addressing any concerns. Help your group members understand that if certain steps are uncomfortable right now, that's okay. Encourage them to do whatever steps are comfortable and to let God speak to them from his Word as they grow in their relationship with him.

Next Session (5 min.) The first four sessions of this study guide have addressed how we as individuals learn from God's Word in our personal relationship with him. In our next session we will be looking at how God's Word speaks to us as his family, as the church, as the body of Christ. Jesus' prayer in John 17 is for all his followers, as individuals and also as a collective group. Ask your group members to look for what Jesus says concerning their relationship to each other.

Close in Prayer (10 min.) Depending on time, you may want to pray for your group or you may want the members to pray for each other in partnerships. Be sure each group member is prayed for individually by name for his or her personal needs this week. In anticipation of the next session's materials, pray for the unity of your group and how you are relating to each other.

Session 5. Scripture & Community.
Introduce the Session (1 min.) Go over the purpose and goal.

Purpose: The purpose of this session is to understand and appreciate how God relates to us through his Word in our interpersonal relationships.

Goal: To develop our confidence in building trusting relationships as we experience the truths of God's Word.

Because many relationships in our lives are strained or at a surface level, the truths of this lesson may be difficult to comprehend or accept. You may want to take a few minutes at the beginning of your time together to discuss one good relationship each one has and what makes it good, and one difficult relationship each one has and what makes it difficult. God's principles on relationships in Scripture relate to all situations; however, for the purpose of this session, help your group focus on your relationships within the group.

Establishing Base Camp (10 min.) Discuss the questions listed. Try to focus this time on the positive elements of your group relationships. If some of the members don't get along with each other and it comes out at this time, that's okay. Encourage them to talk together in private, as in my friend's group, perhaps in a different room or at another time in the near future. It is best not to process disagreements between individuals in the group. However, it is good for a group to hear the resulting apologies and to experience the healing of relationships. Then the group can celebrate together.

I recently had this experience with a member of one of my small groups. Some wounded feelings toward me became evident in our meeting. Unfortunately I began to process them with her in the group meeting. Later we got together to talk about her hurts, and we both came to the group the next time with our apologies for each other as well as for causing awkwardness in the group. Our confession and apologies before the group brought healing in all of our relationships. This is hard to go through but worth it when the healing comes.

Mapping the Trail (10 min.) Read Ecclesiastes 4:9-13 together. Discuss the reasons why two are better than one. How do these reasons relate to your group? Let each member of your group answer the questions listed. For the sake of time, if your group is larger than four or five people, you may want to answer these questions with partners or in groups of three people.

Some people are more inclined toward making decisions and facing trials alone. If some of your group members have difficulty answering these questions, that's okay. Help them to feel safe in the revelation of their lives. As you go through this session, they may express why they have difficulty in this area and that they do desire a close friend to share their life.

Beginning the Ascent (30 min.) If your group members have not read through this section, read through it together and comment as you read or summarize it for them. You may want to read the various texts if your group members are not familiar with the biblical stories.

As you define community, talk about the feelings and expectations your group members have. Talk about their experiences with community or with a lack of community in their lives. What produces biblical, Christ-honoring community and what are the reasons for lack of community in their lives?

Read John 17 aloud. After you have read through this prayer, point out the eight elements in their specific verses. Discuss these elements, what they mean and how they are experienced in your group. Discuss the thoughts and feelings of your group members about these truths.

Refer to the pullout and "Gaining a Foothold." Ask for comments from your group members.

 Trailmarkers (10 min.) Follow the instructions given in this section.

Teamwork (15 min.) Again, the instructions in this section are self-explanatory. Choose one of the ways to create this affirmation time. (You may want to have a couple boxes of tissues available because this will be a very meaningful time in your group when hearts are touched quite deeply.) It is not very often that we receive kind words from others. It will be surprising what each one says to each other person.

Reaching the Summit (5 min.) Use this time to let the emotions of the affirmation time settle. You may also want to briefly summarize the eight elements of Jesus' prayer and how you have just experienced the unity Jesus was talking about.

Next Session (5 min.) Encourage your group members to complete the session-six materials before you come together again. You may want to celebrate the conclusion of this study guide in a special way, with treats of some kind, flowers or balloons. If you need people to bring anything for the celebration, remind them at this time.

Close in Prayer (10 min.) Depending on the amount of time available, you may want to pray for your group or you may want the members to pray for each other in partnerships. Be sure each group member is prayed for individually by name for the thoughts expressed during your meeting and for any needs they are facing this week. Continue with prayers of affirmation if that is appropriate.

Session 6. Putting It All Together.
Introduce the Session (1 min.) Review the purpose and goal with the group. In this session we will use each of the reading styles to gain insights into Romans 12.

Purpose: This session is designed to bring together all that we have learned in this study guide. In doing this we will see how each of these reading styles will enhance our understanding of a biblical passage so that we will know God better and enjoy applying the truths of Scripture to our everyday lives and decisions.

Goal: To increase our enjoyment of reading and responding to God's love revealed in Scripture.

Establishing Base Camp (10 min.) Discuss the questions listed. The purpose of this segment is to help your group realize that worthwhile experiences in life incorporate many skills and much learning. To get group members started talking about their own experiences, share an area of your life that answers these questions.

Mapping the Trail (10 min.) During this time encourage group members to express their true feelings on each of these questions about the various styles of Bible reading described in this study guide. Some people are readers; others are not. You may have a wide variety of feelings expressed in your group. Celebrate this variety. Let them know that God loves them as they are. Also help them to understand the benefits of reading the Bible so that we can learn what God says about himself and us. With this understanding we can face whatever others say with the confidence of knowing the truth.

Beginning the Ascent (30 min.) Although your group has been experiencing the various reading styles over the past several weeks, it will be helpful to remind them of the description, purpose and benefits of each one. Review each style and allow group members to ask any questions they have for each style.

After sharing thoughts and feelings about each reading style, walk through the "Scripture Reading and Response Exercise" together. Most people should have completed this during the week, but briefly go through the process so that they see again how all the styles can be used when studying a passage.

In groups of four, have each member share their preparation work and their memory verses. It is important to honor the work they have done before coming to this meeting.

Refer to the pullout and "Gaining a Foothold." Ask for comments from your group members. Some group members may feel guilty that their Bible reading times are dry, stagnant or stale. They may think it is their fault and that God just doesn't want to relate with them. To help them understand that this happens to everyone, describe a time when this was true for you. How did you overcome this dryness? Read together the verses in Luke 2:10-11. Let your group members explain how Jesus is our joy and how he has been their joy.

Trailmarkers (10 min.) Follow the instructions given in this section.

 Teamwork (15 min.) Again, the instructions in this section are self-explanatory. For the sake of time, you may want to have only one or two group members share their thoughts and feelings on each of the styles rather than everyone on all styles. This would be a good time to ask if anyone has any questions concerning the various styles. Encourage others to answer these questions from their own reading experiences.

▲ Reaching the Summit (5 min.) Before discussing the questions listed in this section, ask if anyone has questions about Romans 12. This is such a fabulous chapter concerning God's love and our relationships with each other; it is important that the truths of this chapter become applications to our life.

You may want to use the teachings of this chapter on self and relationships as the springboard for discussing the answers to the questions listed. However, you may want instead to let your group members relate their answers to any of these sessions. This is a very good time to affirm what each one has learned.

Next Session (5 min.) Because there is so much to discuss in this material, you may not have time to celebrate your completion of this study guide at this meeting. I encourage you to plan a celebration in the near future, perhaps a dinner or a party.

As you discuss future materials to study, take into account the next step your group needs to take toward spiritual maturity. Perhaps it is a study of a specific book in the Bible. Perhaps it is a study on a particular aspect of the Christian life such as prayer, forgiveness, character development or using spiritual gifts. If you have studied other guides in the Bible 101 series, celebrate and reflect back on all the learning, growth and development. Be sure to consider one of the other guides in the series for the future.

Close in Prayer (10 min.) Pray prayers of celebration and gratitude for God's work in you. And pray for the needs of your group. Be sure each group member is prayed for individually by name for the thoughts expressed during your meeting and for any needs they are facing this week.